Pres...

...

on July 9, 1980
by the
Bahá'is of Davis

CALL TO THE NATIONS

Extracts from the writings of

SHOGHI EFFENDI

Well is it with him who fixeth
his gaze upon the Order
of Bahá'u'lláh... The Báb

BAHÁ'Í WORLD CENTRE

ISBN 0 85398 068 3 (cased)
ISBN 0 85398 069 1 (paper)

Printed in Great Britain
by W & J Mackay Limited, Chatham
in 13 pt Bembo type 1 pt leaded

"It is towards this goal—the goal of a new World Order, Divine in origin, all-embracing in scope, equitable in principle, challenging in its features —that a harassed humanity must strive."

Foreword

Shoghi Effendi, Guardian of the Bahá'í Faith, in exercising his function of interpreting the Bahá'í Revelation, dwelt at great length and with considerable emphasis on the world order enshrined within that Revelation. Early in his ministry, which initiated the Formative Age of the Faith, he alluded to "those priceless elements of that Divine Civilization, the establishment of which is the primary mission of the Bahá'í Faith.", and over the years he indited a series of letters, generally referred to as his World Order letters, unfolding this theme.

The vital necessity of world order is largely acknowledged today but the means to achieve it baffle even its most passionate advocates. Meanwhile the process of disintegration continues unchecked and mankind's condition approaches the stage of despair. At this critical juncture the Universal House of Justice, the international governing body of the Bahá'í Faith, feels moved to proclaim again the meaning and purpose of the Bahá'í message and its pertinence to our very existence on earth. It has therefore selected the following passages from Shoghi Effendi's World Order letters, and offers them as a light and a guidance to all mankind in this dark period of our history, a period, nevertheless, whose distant horizon is brilliant with the promise of that most glorious day of all, foretold and sung throughout the ages by prophets, seers and poets and now actually dawning upon the harassed and desperate children of men.

Contents

Introduction

The fundamental principle enunciated by Bahá'u'lláh, the followers of His Faith firmly believe, is that religious truth is not absolute but relative, that Divine Revelation is a continuous and progressive process, that all the great religions of the world are divine in origin, that their basic principles are in complete harmony, that their aims and purposes are one and the same, that their teachings are but facets of one truth, that their functions are complementary, that they differ only in the non-essential aspects of their doctrines, and that their missions represent successive stages in the spiritual evolution of human society.

The aim of Bahá'u'lláh, the Prophet of this new and great age which humanity has entered . . . is not to destroy but to fulfil the Revelations of the past, to reconcile rather than accentuate the divergencies of the conflicting creeds which disrupt present-day society.

His purpose, far from belittling the station of the

Prophets gone before Him or of whittling down their teachings, is to restate the basic truths which these teachings enshrine in a manner that would conform to the needs, and be in consonance with the capacity, and be applicable to the problems, the ills and perplexities, of the age in which we live. His mission is to proclaim that the ages of the infancy and of the childhood of the human race are past, that the convulsions associated with the present stage of its adolescence are slowly and painfully preparing it to attain the stage of manhood, and are heralding the approach of that Age of Ages when swords will be beaten into ploughshares, when the Kingdom promised by Jesus Christ will have been established, and the peace of the planet definitely and permanently ensured. Nor does Bahá'-u'lláh claim finality for His own Revelation, but rather stipulates that a fuller measure of the truth He has been commissioned by the Almighty to vouchsafe to humanity, at so critical a juncture in its fortunes, must needs be disclosed at future stages in the constant and limitless evolution of mankind.

The Bahá'í Faith upholds the unity of God, recognizes the unity of His Prophets, and inculcates the principle of the oneness and wholeness of the entire human race. It proclaims the necessity and the inevitability of the unification of mankind, asserts that it is gradually approaching, and claims that nothing short of the transmuting spirit of God, working through His chosen Mouthpiece in this day, can ultimately succeed in bringing it about. It, moreover, enjoins upon its followers the primary duty of an unfettered search after truth, condemns all manner of prejudice and superstition, declares the purpose of religion to be the promotion of amity and concord, proclaims its essential harmony with science, and recognizes it as the foremost agency for the pacification and the orderly progress of human society. It unequivocally maintains the principle of equal rights, opportunities and privileges for men and women, insists on compulsory education, eliminates extremes of poverty and wealth, abolishes the institution of priesthood, prohibits slavery, asceticism, mendicancy and monasticism, prescribes monogamy, discourages divorce, emphasizes the necessity of strict obedience to one's government, exalts any work performed in the spirit of service to the level of worship, urges either the creation or the selection of an auxiliary international language, and delineates the outlines of those institutions that must establish and perpetuate the general peace of mankind.

The Bahá'í Faith revolves around three central Figures, the first of whom was a youth, a native of Shíráz, named Mírzá 'Alí-Muḥammad, known as the Báb (Gate), who in May 1844, at the age of twenty-five, advanced the claim of being the Herald Who according to the sacred Scriptures of previous Dispensations, must needs announce and prepare the way for the advent of One greater than Himself, Whose mission would be, according to those same Scriptures, to inaugurate an era of righteousness and peace, an era that would be hailed as the consummation of all previous Dispensations, and initiate a new cycle in the religious history of mankind. Swift and severe persecution, launched by the organized forces of Church and State in His native land, precipitated successively His arrest, His exile to the mountains of Ádhirbáyján, His imprisonment in the fortresses of Máh-Kú and Chihríq, and His execution, in July 1850, by a firing squad in the public square of Tabríz. No less than twenty thousand of his followers were put to death with such barbarous cruelty as to evoke the warm sympathy and the unqualified admiration of a number of Western writers, diplomats, travellers and scholars, some of whom were witnesses of these abominable outrages, and were moved to record them in their books and diaries.

Mírzá Ḥusayn-'Alí, surnamed Bahá'u'lláh (the Glory of God), a native of Mázindarán, Whose advent the Báb had foretold, was assailed by those same forces of ignorance and fanaticism, was imprisoned in Ṭihrán, was banished, in 1852, from His native land to Baghdád, and thence to Constantinople and Adrianople, and finally to the prison city of 'Akká, where He remained incarcerated for no less than

xiv

twenty-four years, and in whose neighbourhood He passed away in 1892. In the course of His banishment, and particularly in Adrianople and 'Akká, He formulated the laws and ordinances of His Dispensation, expounded, in over a hundred volumes, the principles of His Faith, proclaimed His Message to the kings and rulers of both the East and the West, both Christian and Muslim, addressed the Pope, the Caliph of Islám, the Chief Magistrates of the Republics of the American continent, the entire Christian sacerdotal order, the leaders of S̲h̲í'ih and Sunní Islám, and the high priests of the Zoroastrian religion. In these writings He proclaimed His Revelation, summoned those whom He addressed to heed His call and espouse His Faith, warned them of the consequences of their refusal, and denounced, in some cases, their arrogance and tyranny.

His eldest son, 'Abbás Effendi, known as 'Abdu'l-Bahá (the Servant of Bahá), appointed by Him as His lawful successor and the authorized interpreter of His teachings, Who since early childhood had been closely associated with His Father, and shared His exile and tribulations, remained a prisoner until 1908, when, as a result of the Young Turk Revolution, He was released from His confinement. Establishing His residence in Haifa, He embarked soon after on His three-year journey to Egypt, Europe and North America, in the course of which He expounded before vast audiences, the teachings of His Father and predicted the approach of that catastrophe that was soon to befall mankind. He returned to His home on the eve of the first World War, in the course of which He was exposed to constant danger, until the liberation of Palestine by the forces under the command of General Allenby, who extended the utmost consideration to Him and to the small band of His fellow-exiles in 'Akká and Haifa. In 1921 He passed away, and was buried in a vault in the mausoleum erected on Mount Carmel, at the express instruction of Bahá'u'lláh, for the remains of the Báb, which had previously been transferred from Tabríz to the Holy Land after having been preserved and concealed for no less than sixty years.

The passing of 'Abdu'l-Bahá marked the termination of the first and Heroic Age of the Bahá'í Faith and signalized the opening of the Formative Age destined to witness the gradual emergence of its Administrative Order, whose establishment had been foretold by the Báb, whose laws were revealed by Bahá'u'lláh, whose outlines were delineated by 'Abdu'l-Bahá in His Will and Testament, and whose foundations are now being laid by the national and local councils which are elected by the professed adherents of the Faith. . . .

This Administrative Order, unlike the systems evolved after the death of the Founders of the various religions, is divine in origin, rests securely on the laws, the precepts, the ordinances and institutions which the Founder of the Faith has Himself specifically laid down and unequivocally established, and functions in strict accordance with the interpretations of the authorized Interpreters of its holy scriptures. Though fiercely assailed, ever since its inception, it has, by virtue of its character, unique in the annals of the world's religious history, succeeded in maintaining the unity of the diversified and far-flung body of its supporters, and enabled them to launch, unitedly and systematically, enterprises in both hemispheres, designed to extend its limits and consolidate its administrative institutions.

The Faith which this order serves, safeguards and promotes, is, it should be noted in this connection, essentially supernatural, supranational, entirely non-political, non-partisan, and diametrically opposed to any policy or school of thought that seeks to exalt any particular race, class or nation. It is free from any form of ecclesiasticism, has neither priesthood nor rituals, and is supported exclusively by voluntary contributions made by its avowed adherents. Though loyal to their respective governments, though imbued with the love of their own country, and anxious to promote, at all times, its best interests, the followers of the Bahá'í Faith, nevertheless, viewing mankind as one entity, and profoundly attached to its vital interests, will not hesitate to subordinate every particular interest, be it personal, regional or national, to the overriding interests of the generality of mankind, knowing full well that in a world of interdependent peoples and nations the advantage of the part is best to be reached by the advantage of the whole, and that no lasting result can be achieved by any of the component parts if the general interests of the entity itself are neglected. . . .

I

Humanity's Ordeal

A tempest, unprecedented in its violence, unpredictable in its course, catastrophic in its immediate effects, unimaginably glorious in its ultimate consequences, is at present sweeping the face of the earth.[1] Its driving power is remorselessly gaining in range and momentum. Its cleansing force, however much undetected, is increasing with every passing day. Humanity, gripped in the clutches of its devastating power, is smitten by the evidences of its resistless fury. It can neither perceive its origin, nor probe its significance, nor discern its outcome. Bewildered, agonized and helpless, it watches this great and mighty wind of God invading the remotest and fairest regions of the earth, rocking its foundations, deranging its equilibrium, sundering its nations, disrupting the homes of its peoples, wasting its cities, driving into exile its kings, pulling down its bulwarks, uprooting its institutions, dimming its light, and harrowing up the souls

[1] Written in March 1941.

of its inhabitants....

The powerful operations of this titanic upheaval are comprehensible to none except such as have recognized the claims of both Bahá'u'lláh and the Báb. Their followers know full well whence it comes, and what it will ultimately lead to. Though ignorant of how far it will reach, they clearly recognize its genesis, are aware of its direction, acknowledge its necessity, observe confidently its mysterious processes, ardently pray for the mitigation of its severity, intelligently labour to assuage its fury, and anticipate, with un-dimmed vision, the consummation of the fears and the hopes it must necessarily engender.

This judgement of God, as viewed by those who have recognized Bahá'u'lláh as His Mouthpiece and His greatest Messenger on earth, is both a retributory calamity and an act of holy and supreme discipline. It is at once a visitation from God and a cleansing process for all mankind. Its fires punish the perversity of the human race, and weld its component parts into one organic, indivisible, world–embracing community....

"Bestir yourselves, O people," is, on the one hand, the ominous warning sounded by Bahá'u'lláh Him-self, *"in anticipation of the days of Divine Justice, for the promised hour is now come."* *"Abandon that which ye possess, and seize that which God, Who layeth low the necks of men, hath brought. Know ye of a certainty that if ye turn not back from that which ye have committed, chastise-*

2

ment will overtake you on every side, and ye shall behold things more grievous than that which ye beheld aforetime." And again: "We have fixed a time for you, O people! If ye fail, at the appointed hour, to turn towards God, He, verily, will lay violent hold on you, and will cause grievous afflictions to assail you from every direction." ...

"The whole earth," Bahá'u'lláh, on the other hand, forecasting the bright future in store for a world now wrapped in darkness, emphatically asserts, "is now in a state of pregnancy. The day is approaching when it will have yielded its noblest fruits, when from it will have sprung forth the loftiest trees, the most enchanting blossoms, the most heavenly blessings." "The time is approaching when every created thing will have cast its burden. Glorified be God Who hath vouchsafed this grace that encompasseth all things, whether seen or unseen!" "These great oppressions," He, moreover, foreshadowing humanity's golden age, has written, "are preparing it for the advent of the Most Great Justice." This Most Great Justice is indeed the Justice upon which the structure of the Most Great Peace can alone, and must eventually, rest, while the Most Great Peace will, in turn usher in that Most Great, that World Civilization which shall remain for ever associated with Him Who beareth the Most Great Name. ...

Well nigh a hundred years have elapsed since the Revelation of Bahá'u'lláh dawned upon the world—a Revelation, the nature of which, as affirmed by Himself, "*none among the Manifestations of old, except to a prescribed degree, hath ever completely apprehended.*" For a whole century God has respited mankind, that it might acknowledge the Founder of such a Revelation, espouse His Cause, proclaim His greatness, and establish His Order. In a hundred volumes, the repositories of priceless precepts, mighty laws, unique principles, impassioned exhortations, reiterated warnings, amazing prophecies, sublime invocations, and weighty commentaries, the Bearer of such a Message has proclaimed, as no Prophet before Him has done, the Mission with which God had entrusted Him. To emperors, kings, princes and potentates, to rulers, governments, clergy and peoples, whether of the East or of the West, whether Christian, Jew, Muslim, or Zoroastrian, He addressed, for well-nigh fifty years, and in the most tragic circumstances, these priceless pearls of knowledge and wisdom that lay hid within the ocean of His matchless utterance. Forsaking fame and fortune, accepting imprisonment and exile, careless of ostracism and obloquy, submitting to physical indignities and cruel deprivations, He, the Vicegerent of God on earth, suffered Himself to be banished from place to place and from country to country. . . . "*We verily,*" He Himself has testified, "*have not fallen short of Our duty to exhort men, and to deliver that whereunto I was bidden by God, the Almighty, the All-Praised. Had they hearkened unto Me, they would have beheld the earth*

4

another earth." And again: *"Is there any excuse left for any one in this Revelation? No, by God, the Lord of the Mighty Throne! My signs have encompassed the earth, and My power enveloped all mankind, and yet the people are wrapped in a strange sleep!"*

How—we may well ask ourselves—has the world, the object of such Divine solicitude, repaid Him Who sacrificed His all for its sake? What manner of welcome did it accord Him, and what response did His call evoke? A clamour, unparalleled in the history of Shí'ih Islám, greeted, in the land of its birth, the infant light of the Faith. . . . A persecution, kindling a courage which, as attested by no less eminent an authority than the late Lord Curzon of Kedleston, has been unsurpassed by that which the fires of Smithfield evoked, mowed down, with tragic swiftness, no less than twenty thousand of its heroic adherents, who refused to barter their newly-born faith for the fleeting honours and security of a mortal life. . . .

Unmitigated indifference on the part of men of eminence and rank; unrelenting hatred shown by the ecclesiastical dignitaries of the Faith from which it had sprung; the scornful derision of the people among whom it was born; the utter contempt which most of those kings and rulers who had been addressed by its Author manifested towards it; the condemnations pronounced, the threats hurled, and the banishments decreed by those under whose sway it arose and first spread; the distortion to which its principles and laws were subjected by the envious and the malicious, in lands and among peoples far beyond the country of its origin—all these are but the evidences of the treatment meted out by a generation sunk in self-content, careless of its God, and oblivious of the omens, prophecies, warnings and admonitions revealed by His Messengers. . . .

What, then—might we not consider—has, in the face of so complete and ignominious a rejection, happened, and is still happening, in the course, and particularly in the closing years, of this, the first Bahá'í century, a century fraught with such tumultuous sufferings and violent outrages for the persecuted Faith of Bahá'u'lláh? Empires fallen in dust, kingdoms subverted, dynasties extinguished, royalty besmirched, kings assassinated, poisoned, driven into exile, subjugated in their own realms, whilst the few remaining thrones are trembling with the repercussions of the fall of their fellows. . . . Surely, no man, contemplating dispassionately the manifestations of this relentless revolutionizing process, within comparatively so short a time, can escape the conclusion that the last hundred years may well be regarded, in so far as the fortunes of royalty are concerned, as one of the most cataclysmic periods in the annals of mankind. . . .

The decline in the fortunes of the crowned wielders of temporal power has been paralleled by a no less

6

startling deterioration in the influence exercised by the world's spiritual leaders. The colossal events that have heralded the dissolution of so many kingdoms and empires have almost synchronized with the crumbling of the seemingly inviolable strongholds of religious orthodoxy. That same process which, swiftly and tragically, sealed the doom of kings and emperors, and extinguished their dynasties, has operated in the case of the ecclesiastical leaders of both Christianity and Islám, damaging their prestige, and, in some cases, overthrowing their highest institutions. "*Power hath been seized*" indeed, from both "*kings and ecclesiastics*". The glory of the former has been eclipsed, the power of the latter irretrievably lost. . . .

That the solidarity of some of these institutions has been irretrievably shattered is too apparent for any intelligent observer to mistake or deny. The cleavage between the fundamentalists and the liberals among their adherents is continually widening. Their creeds and dogmas have been watered down, and in certain instances ignored and discarded. Their hold upon human conduct is loosening, and the personnel of their ministries is dwindling in number and in influence. The timidity and insincerity of their preachers are, in several instances, being exposed. Their endowments have, in some countries, disappeared, and the force of their religious training has declined. Their temples have been partly deserted and destroyed, and an oblivion of God, of His teachings and of His Purpose, has enfeebled and heaped humiliation upon them. . . .

The signs of moral downfall, as distinct from the evidences of decay in religious institutions, would appear to be no less noticeable and significant. . . . In whichever direction we turn our gaze, no matter how cursory our observation of the doings and sayings of the present generation, we cannot fail to be struck by the evidences of moral decadence which, in their individual lives no less than in their collective capacity, men and women around us exhibit.

There can be no doubt that the decline of religion as a social force, of which the deterioration of religious institutions is but an external phenomenon, is chiefly responsible for so grave, so conspicuous an evil. "*Religion,*" writes Bahá'u'lláh, "*is the greatest of all means for the establishment of order in the world and for the peaceful contentment of all that dwell therein. The weakening of the pillars of religion hath strengthened the hands of the ignorant and made them bold and arrogant. Verily I say, whatsoever hath lowered the lofty station of religion hath increased the waywardness of the wicked, and the result cannot be but anarchy.*" "*Religion,*" He, in another Tablet, has stated, "*is a radiant light and an impregnable stronghold for the protection and welfare of the peoples of*

8

the world, for the fear of God impelleth man to hold fast to that which is good, and shun all evil. Should the lamp of religion be obscured, chaos and confusion will ensue, and the lights of fairness, of justice, of tranquillity and peace cease to shine." ...

Such, we might well admit, is the state which individuals and institutions alike are approaching. *"No two men,"* Bahá'u'lláh, lamenting the plight of an erring humanity, has written, *"can be found who may be said to be outwardly and inwardly united. The evidences of discord and malice are apparent everywhere, though all were made for harmony and union." "How long,"* He, in the same Tablet, exclaims, *"will humanity persist in its waywardness? How long will injustice continue? How long is chaos and confusion to reign amongst men? How long will discord agitate the face of society? The winds of despair are, alas, blowing from every direction, and the strife that divideth and afflicteth the human race is daily increasing."*

The recrudescence of religious intolerance, of racial animosity, and of patriotic arrogance; the increasing evidences of selfishness, of suspicion, of fear and of fraud; the spread of terrorism, of lawlessness, of drunkenness and of crime; the unquenchable thirst for, and the feverish pursuit after, earthly vanities, riches and pleasures; the weakening of family solidarity; the laxity in parental control; the lapse into luxurious indulgence; the irresponsible attitude towards marriage and the consequent rising tide of

9

divorce; the degeneracy of art and music, the infection of literature, and the corruption of the press; the extension of the influence and activities of those "prophets of decadence" who advocate companionate marriage, who preach the philosophy of nudism, who call modesty an intellectual fiction, who refuse to regard the procreation of children as the sacred and primary purpose of marriage, who denounce religion as an opiate of the people, who would, if given free rein, lead back the human race to barbarism, chaos, and ultimate extinction—these appear as the outstanding characteristics of a decadent society, a society that must be either reborn or perish. . . .

Let none, however, mistake my purpose, or misrepresent this cardinal truth which is of the essence of the Faith of Bahá'u'lláh. The divine origin of all the Prophets of God . . . is unreservedly and unshakeably upheld by each and every follower of the Bahá'í religion. The fundamental unity of these Messengers of God is clearly recognized, the continuity of their Revelations is affirmed, the God-given authority and correlative character of their Books is admitted, the singleness of their aims and purposes is proclaimed, the uniqueness of their influence emphasized, the ultimate reconciliation of their teachings and followers taught and anticipated. "*They all*," according to

Bahá'u'lláh's testimony, "*abide in the same tabernacle, soar in the same heaven, are seated upon the same throne, utter the same speech, and proclaim the same Faith.*"

The Faith standing identified with the name of Bahá'u'lláh disclaims any intention to belittle any of the Prophets gone before Him, to whittle down any of their teachings, to obscure, however slightly, the radiance of their Revelations, to oust them from the hearts of their followers, to abrogate the fundamentals of their doctrines, to discard any of their revealed Books, or to suppress the legitimate aspirations of their adherents. Repudiating the claim of any religion to be the final revelation of God to man, disclaiming finality for His own Revelation, Bahá'u'lláh inculcates the basic principle of the relativity of religious truth, the continuity of Divine Revelation, the progressiveness of religious experience. His aim is to widen the basis of all revealed religions and to unravel the mysteries of their scriptures. He insists on the unqualified recognition of the unity of their purpose, restates the eternal verities they enshrine, coordinates their functions, distinguishes the essential and the authentic from the non-essential and spurious in their teachings, separates the God-given truths from the priest-prompted superstitions, and on this as a basis proclaims the possibility, and even prophesies the inevitability, of their unification, and the consummation of their highest hopes. . . .

Nor should it be thought for a moment that the followers of Bahá'u'lláh either seek to degrade or even belittle the rank of the world's religious leaders, whether Christian, Muslim, or of any other denomination, should their conduct conform to their professions, and be worthy of the position they occupy. "*Those divines,*" Bahá'u'lláh has affirmed, " *. . . who are truly adorned with the ornament of knowledge and of a goodly character are, verily, as a head to the body of the world, and as eyes to the nations. The guidance of men hath, at all times, been and is dependent upon these blessed souls.*" . . .

Bahá'u'lláh, referring to the transformation effected by every Revelation in the ways, thoughts and manners of the people, reveals these words: "*Is not the object of every Revelation to effect a transformation in the whole character of mankind, a transformation that shall manifest itself, both outwardly and inwardly, that shall affect both its inner life and external conditions? For if the character of mankind be not changed, the futility of God's universal Manifestation would be apparent.*"

Did not Christ Himself, addressing His disciples, utter these words: "*I have yet many things to say unto you, but ye cannot bear them now. Howbeit when He, the Spirit of Truth, is come, He will guide you into all truth*"?

From the . . . words of Christ, as attested by the Gospel, every unprejudiced observer will readily apprehend the magnitude of the Faith which Bahá'-u'lláh has revealed, and recognize the staggering weight of the claim He has advanced. . . .

The Faith of Bahá'u'lláh should indeed be regarded, if we wish to be faithful to the tremendous implications of its message, as the culmination of a cycle, the final stage in a series of successive, of preliminary and progressive revelations. These, beginning with Adam and ending with the Báb, have paved the way and anticipated with an ever-increasing emphasis the advent of that Day of Days in which He Who is the Promise of All Ages should be made manifest. . . .

The weight of the potentialities with which this Faith, possessing no peer or equal in the world's spiritual history, and marking the culmination of a universal prophetic cycle, has been endowed, staggers our imagination. The brightness of the millennial glory which it must shed in the fullness of time dazzles our eyes. The magnitude of the shadow which its Author will continue to cast on successive Prophets destined to be raised up after Him eludes our calculation.

Already in the space of less than a century[1] the operation of the mysterious processes generated by its creative spirit has provoked a tumult in human society such as no mind can fathom. Itself undergoing a period of incubation during its primitive age, it has, through the emergence of its slowly-crystallizing system, induced a fermentation in the general life of mankind designed to shake the very foundations of a disordered society, to purify its life-blood, to reorientate and reconstruct its institutions, and shape its final destiny.

To what else can the observant eye or the unprejudiced mind, acquainted with the signs and portents heralding the birth, and accompanying the rise, of the Faith of Bahá'u'lláh ascribe this dire, this planetary upheaval, with its attendant destruction, misery and fear, if not to the emergence of His embryonic World Order, which, as He Himself has unequivocally proclaimed, has *"deranged the equilibrium of the world and revolutionized mankind's ordered life"*? To what agency, if not to the irresistible diffusion of that world-shaking, world-energizing, world-redeeming spirit, which the Báb has affirmed is *"vibrating in the innermost realities of all created things"* can the origins of this portentous crisis, incomprehensible to man, and admittedly unprecedented in the annals of the human race, be attributed? In the convulsions of contemporary society, in the frenzied, world-wide ebullitions of

[1] Written in 1944.

14

men's thoughts, in the fierce antagonisms inflaming races, creeds and classes, in the shipwreck of nations, in the downfall of kings, in the dismemberment of empires, in the extinction of dynasties, in the collapse of ecclesiastical hierarchies, in the deterioration of time-honoured institutions, in the dissolution of ties, secular as well as religious, that had for so long held together the members of the human race—all manifesting themselves with ever-increasing gravity since the outbreak of the first World War that immediately preceded the opening years of the Formative Age of the Faith of Bahá'u'lláh—in these we can readily recognize the evidences of the travail of an age that has sustained the impact of His Revelation, that has ignored His summons, and is now labouring to be delivered of its burden, as a direct consequence of the impulse communicated to it by the generative, the purifying, the transmuting influence of His Spirit. . . .

Mysteriously, slowly, and resistlessly God accomplishes His design, though the sight that meets our eyes in this day be the spectacle of a world hopelessly entangled in its own meshes, utterly careless of the Voice which, for a century, has been calling it to God, and miserably subservient to the siren voices which are attempting to lure it into the vast abyss.

God's purpose is none other than to usher in, in

ways He alone can bring about, and the full significance of which He alone can fathom, the Great, the Golden Age of a long-divided, a long-afflicted humanity. Its present state, indeed even its immediate future, is dark, distressingly dark. Its distant future, however, is radiant, gloriously radiant—so radiant that no eye can visualize it.

II

The Oneness of Mankind

Humanity, whether viewed in the light of man's individual conduct or in the existing relationships between organized communities and nations, has, alas, strayed too far and suffered too great a decline to be redeemed through the unaided efforts of the best among its recognized rulers and statesmen— however disinterested their motives, however concerted their action, however unsparing in their zeal and devotion to its cause. No scheme which the calculations of the highest statesmanship may yet devise; no doctrine which the most distinguished exponents of economic theory may hope to advance; no principle which the most ardent of moralists may strive to inculcate, can provide, in the last resort, adequate foundations upon which the future of a distracted world can be built.

No appeal for mutual tolerance which the worldly-wise might raise, however compelling and insistent, can calm its passions or help restore its vigour. Nor would any general scheme of mere organized international cooperation, in whatever sphere of human activity, however ingenious in conception, or extensive in scope, succeed in removing the root cause of the evil that has so rudely upset the equilibrium of present-day society. Not even, I venture to assert, would the very act of devising the machinery required for the political and economic unification of the world—a principle that has been increasingly advocated in recent times—provide in itself the antidote against the poison that is steadily undermining the vigour of organized peoples and nations.

What else, might we not confidently affirm, but the unreserved acceptance of the Divine Programme enunciated, with such simplicity and force as far back as sixty years ago,[1] by Bahá'u'lláh, embodying in its essentials God's divinely appointed scheme for the unification of mankind in this age, coupled with an indomitable conviction in the unfailing efficacy of each and all of its provisions, is eventually capable of withstanding the forces of internal disintegration which, if unchecked, must needs continue to eat into the vitals of a despairing society. It is towards this goal—the goal of a new World Order, Divine in origin, all-embracing in scope, equitable in principle, challenging in its features—that a harassed humanity must strive.

To claim to have grasped all the implications of

[1] Written in 1931.

Bahá'u'lláh's prodigious scheme for world-wide human solidarity, or to have fathomed its import, would be presumptuous on the part of even the declared supporters of His Faith. To attempt to visualize it in all its possibilities, to estimate its future benefits, to picture its glory, would be premature at even so advanced a stage in the evolution of mankind.

All we can reasonably venture to attempt is to strive to obtain a glimpse of the first streaks of the promised Dawn that must, in the fullness of time, chase away the gloom that has encircled humanity. All we can do is to point out, in their broadest outlines, what appears to us to be the guiding principles underlying the World Order of Bahá'u'lláh. . . .

That the unrest and suffering afflicting the mass of mankind are in no small measure the direct consequences of the World War[1] and are attributable to the unwisdom and short-sightedness of the framers of the Peace Treaties only a biased mind can refuse to admit. . . . It would be idle, however, to contend that the war, with all the losses it involved, the passions it aroused and the grievances it left behind, has solely been responsible for the unprecedented confusion into which almost every section of the civilized world is plunged at present. Is it not a fact—and this is the central idea I desire to emphasize—that the fundamental cause of this world unrest is attributable, not

[1] Written in 1931 and refers to the first World War.

so much to the consequences of what must sooner or later come to be regarded as a transitory dislocation in the affairs of a continually changing world, but rather to the failure of those into whose hands the immediate destinies of peoples and nations have been committed, to adjust their systems of economic and political institutions to the imperative needs of a rapidly evolving age? Are not these intermittent crises that convulse present-day society due primarily to the lamentable inability of the world's recognized leaders to read aright the signs of the times, to rid themselves once for all of their preconceived ideas and fettering creeds, and to reshape the machinery of their respective governments according to those standards that are implicit in Bahá'u'lláh's supreme declaration of the Oneness of Mankind—the chief and distinguishing feature of the Faith He proclaimed? For the principle of the Oneness of Mankind, the corner-stone of Bahá'u'lláh's world-embracing dominion, implies nothing more nor less than the enforcement of His scheme for the unification of the world—the scheme to which we have already referred. "*In every Dispensation,*" writes 'Abdu'l-Bahá, "*the light of Divine Guidance has been focussed upon one central theme. . . . In this wondrous Revelation, this glorious century, the foundation of the Faith of God and the distinguishing feature of His Law is the consciousness of the Oneness of Mankind.*"

How pathetic indeed are the efforts of those leaders

of human institutions who, in utter disregard of the spirit of the age, are striving to adjust national processes, suited to the ancient days of self-contained nations, to an age which must either achieve the unity of the world, as adumbrated by Bahá'u'lláh, or perish. At so critical an hour in the history of civilization it behoves the leaders of all the nations of the world, great and small, whether in the East or in the West, whether victors or vanquished, to give heed to the clarion call of Bahá'u'lláh and, thoroughly imbued with a sense of world solidarity, the *sine qua non* of loyalty to His Cause, arise manfully to carry out in its entirety the one remedial scheme He, the Divine Physician, has prescribed for an ailing humanity. Let them discard, once for all, every preconceived idea, every national prejudice, and give heed to the sublime counsel of 'Abdu'l-Bahá, the authorized Expounder of His teachings. "*You can best serve your country*", was 'Abdu'l-Bahá's rejoinder to a high official in the service of the federal government of the United States of America, who had questioned Him as to the best manner in which he could promote the interests of his government and people, "*if you strive, in your capacity as a citizen of the world, to assist in the eventual application of the principle of federalism underlying the government of your own country to the relationships now existing between the peoples and nations of the world.*"

In *The Secret of Divine Civilization,* 'Abdu'l-Bahá's

outstanding contribution to the future reorganization of the world, we read the following:

"*True civilization will unfurl its banner in the midmost heart of the world whenever a certain number of its distinguished and high-minded sovereigns—the shining exemplars of devotion and determination—shall, for the good and happiness of all mankind, arise, with firm resolve and clear vision, to establish the Cause of Universal Peace. They must make the Cause of Peace the object of general consultation, and seek by every means in their power to establish a Union of the nations of the world. They must conclude a binding treaty and establish a covenant, the provisions of which shall be sound, inviolable and definite. They must proclaim it to all the world and obtain for it the sanction of all the human race. This supreme and noble undertaking—the real source of the peace and well-being of all the world—should be regarded as sacred by all that dwell on earth. All the forces of humanity must be mobilized to ensure the stability and permanence of this Most Great Covenant. In this all-embracing Pact the limits and frontiers of each and every nation should be clearly fixed, the principles underlying the relations of governments towards one another definitely laid down, and all international agreements and obligations ascertained. In like manner, the size of the armaments of every government should be strictly limited, for if the preparations for war and the military forces of any nation should be allowed to increase, they will arouse the suspicion of others. The fundamental*

22

principle underlying this solemn Pact should be so fixed that if any government later violate any one of its provisions, all the governments on earth should arise to reduce it to utter submission, nay the human race as a whole should resolve, with every power at its disposal, to destroy that government. Should this greatest of all remedies be applied to the sick body of the world, it will assuredly recover from its ills and will remain eternally safe and secure."

"A few," He further adds, *"unaware of the power latent in human endeavour, consider this matter as highly impracticable, nay even beyond the scope of man's utmost efforts. Such is not the case, however. On the contrary, thanks to the unfailing grace of God, the loving-kindness of His favoured ones, the unrivalled endeavours of wise and capable souls, and the thoughts and ideas of the peerless leaders of this age, nothing whatsoever can be regarded as unattainable. Endeavour, ceaseless endeavour, is required. Nothing short of an indomitable determination can possibly achieve it. Many a cause which past ages have regarded as purely visionary, yet in this day has become most easy and practicable. Why should this most great and lofty cause— the day-star of the firmament of true civilization and the cause of the glory, the advancement, the well-being and the success of all humanity—be regarded as impossible of achievement? Surely the day will come when its beauteous light shall shed illumination upon the assemblage of man."*

In one of His Tablets 'Abdu'l-Bahá, elucidating further His noble theme, reveals the following:

"*In cycles gone by, though harmony was established, yet, owing to the absence of means, the unity of all mankind could not have been achieved. Continents remained widely divided, nay even among the peoples of one and the same continent association and interchange of thought were well nigh impossible. Consequently intercourse, understanding and unity amongst all the peoples and kindreds of the earth were unattainable. In this day, however, means of communication have multiplied, and the five continents of the earth have virtually merged into one. . . . In like manner all the members of the human family, whether peoples or governments, cities or villages, have become increasingly interdependent. For none is self-sufficiency any longer possible, inasmuch as political ties unite all peoples and nations, and the bonds of trade and industry, of agriculture and education, are being strengthened every day. Hence the unity of all mankind can in this day be achieved. Verily this is none other but one of the wonders of this wondrous age, this glorious century. Of this past ages have been deprived, for this century—the century of light—has been endowed with unique and unprecedented glory, power and illumination. Hence the miraculous unfolding of a fresh marvel every day. Eventually it will be seen how bright its candles will burn in the assemblage of man.*

"*Behold how its light is now dawning upon the world's darkened horizon. The first candle is unity in the political realm, the early glimmerings of which can now be discerned. The second candle is unity of thought in world undertakings,*

24

the consummation of which will ere long be witnessed. The third candle is unity in freedom which will surely come to pass. The fourth candle is unity in religion which is the corner-stone of the foundation itself, and which, by the power of God, will be revealed in all its splendour. The fifth candle is the unity of nations—a unity which in this century will be securely established, causing all the peoples of the world to regard themselves as citizens of one common fatherland. The sixth candle is unity of races, making of all that dwell on earth peoples and kindreds of one race. The seventh candle is unity of language, i.e., the choice of a universal tongue in which all peoples will be instructed and converse. Each and every one of these will inevitably come to pass, inasmuch as the power of the Kingdom of God will aid and assist in their realization."

Over sixty years ago[1], in His Tablet to Queen Victoria, Bahá'u'lláh, addressing "the concourse of the rulers of the earth," revealed the following:

"Take ye counsel together, and let your concern be only for that which profiteth mankind and bettereth the condition thereof. . . . Regard the world as the human body which, though created whole and perfect, has been afflicted, through divers causes, with grave ills and maladies. Not for one day did it rest, nay its sicknesses waxed more severe, as it fell under the treatment of unskilled physicians who have spurred on the steed of their worldly desires and have erred

[1] Now over a century; the Tablet to Queen Victoria was written about 1870.

grievously. And if at one time, through the care of an able physician, a member of that body was healed, the rest remained afflicted as before." . . .

In a further passage Bahá'u'lláh adds these words:

"We see you adding every year unto your expenditures and laying the burden thereof on the people whom ye rule; this verily is naught but grievous injustice. Fear the sighs and tears of this Wronged One, and burden not your peoples beyond that which they can endure. . . . Be reconciled among yourselves, that ye may need armaments no more save in a measure to safeguard your territories and dominions. Be united, O concourse of the sovereigns of the world, for thereby will the tempest of discord be stilled amongst you and your peoples find rest. Should any one among you take up arms against another, rise ye all against him, for this is naught but manifest justice."

What else could these weighty words signify if they did not point to the inevitable curtailment of unfettered national sovereignty as an indispensable preliminary to the formation of the future Commonwealth of all the nations of the world? Some form of a world super-state must needs be evolved, in whose favour all the nations of the world will have willingly ceded every claim to make war, certain rights to impose taxation and all rights to maintain armaments, except for purposes of maintaining internal order within their respective dominions. Such a state will have to include within its orbit an International

Executive adequate to enforce supreme and unchallengeable authority on every recalcitrant member of the commonwealth; a World Parliament whose members shall be elected by the people in their respective countries and whose election shall be confirmed by their respective governments; and a Supreme Tribunal whose judgement will have a binding effect even in such cases where the parties concerned did not voluntarily agree to submit their case to its consideration. A world community in which all economic barriers will have been permanently demolished and the interdependence of Capital and Labour definitely recognized; in which the clamour of religious fanaticism and strife will have been forever stilled; in which the flame of racial animosity will have been finally extinguished; in which a single code of international law—the product of the considered judgement of the world's federated representatives—shall have as its sanction the instant and coercive intervention of the combined forces of the federated units; and finally a world community in which the fury of a capricious and militant nationalism will have been transmuted into an abiding consciousness of world citizenship—such indeed appears, in its broadest outline, the Order anticipated by Bahá'u'lláh, an Order that shall come to be regarded as the fairest fruit of a slowly maturing age.

"*The Tabernacle of Unity,*" Bahá'u'lláh proclaims in His message to all mankind, "*has been raised; regard ye*

*not one another as strangers. . . . Of one tree are all ye the
fruit and of one bough the leaves. . . . The world is but one
country and mankind its citizens. . . . Let not a man glory in
that he loves his country; let him rather glory in this, that
he loves his kind."*

Let there be no misgivings as to the animating purpose of the world-wide Law of Bahá'u'lláh. Far from
aiming at the subversion of the existing foundations
of society, it seeks to broaden its basis, to remould its
institutions in a manner consonant with the needs of
an ever-changing world. It can conflict with no
legitimate allegiances, nor can it undermine essential
loyalties. Its purpose is neither to stifle the flame of a
sane and intelligent patriotism in men's hearts, nor to
abolish the system of national autonomy so essential
if the evils of excessive centralization are to be avoided.
It does not ignore, nor does it attempt to suppress, the
diversity of ethnical origins, of climate, of history, of
language and tradition, of thought and habit, that
differentiate the peoples and nations of the world. It
calls for a wider loyalty, for a larger aspiration than
any that has animated the human race. It insists upon
the subordination of national impulses and interests to
the imperative claims of a unified world. It repudiates
excessive centralization on one hand, and disclaims all
attempts at uniformity on the other. Its watchword is
unity in diversity such as 'Abdu'l-Bahá Himself has
explained:

"*Consider the flowers of a garden. Though differing in kind, colour, form and shape, yet, inasmuch as they are refreshed by the waters of one spring, revived by the breath of one wind, invigorated by the rays of one sun, this diversity increaseth their charm and addeth unto their beauty. How unpleasing to the eye if all the flowers and plants, the leaves and blossoms, the fruit, the branches and the trees of that garden were all of the same shape and colour! Diversity of hues, form and shape enricheth and adorneth the garden, and heighteneth the effect thereof. In like manner, when divers shades of thought, temperament and character are brought together under the power and influence of one central agency, the beauty and glory of human perfection will be revealed and made manifest. Naught but the celestial potency of the Word of God, which ruleth and transcendeth the realities of all things, is capable of harmonizing the divergent thoughts, sentiments, ideas and convictions of the children of men.*"

The call of Bahá'u'lláh is primarily directed against all forms of provincialism, all insularities and pre-judices. If long-cherished ideals and time-honoured institutions, if certain social assumptions and religious formulae have ceased to promote the welfare of the generality of mankind, if they no longer minister to the needs of a continually evolving humanity, let them be swept away and relegated to the limbo of obsoles-cent and forgotten doctrines. Why should these, in a world subject to the immutable law of change and decay, be exempt from the deterioration that must needs overtake every human institution? For legal standards, political and economic theories are solely designed to safeguard the interests of humanity as a whole, and not humanity to be crucified for the preservation of the integrity of any particular law or doctrine.

Let there be no mistake. The principle of the Oneness of Mankind—the pivot round which all the teachings of Bahá'u'lláh revolve—is no mere outburst of ignorant emotionalism or an expression of vague and pious hope. Its appeal is not to be merely identified with a reawakening of the spirit of brotherhood and good-will among men, nor does it aim solely at the fostering of harmonious cooperation among individual peoples and nations. Its implications are deeper, its claims greater than any which the Prophets of old were allowed to advance. Its message is applicable not only to the individual, but concerns itself primarily with the nature of those essential relationships that must bind all the states and nations as members of one human family. It does not constitute merely the enunciation of an ideal, but stands inseparably associated with an institution adequate to embody its truth, demonstrate its validity, and perpetuate its influence. It implies an organic change in the structure of present-day society, a change such as the world has not yet experienced. It constitutes a challenge, at once bold and universal, to outworn shibboleths of national creeds—creeds that have had their day and which must, in the ordinary course of events as shaped and controlled by Providence, give way to a new gospel, fundamentally different from, and infinitely superior to, what the world has already conceived. It calls for no less than the reconstruction and the demilitarization of the whole civilized world —a world organically unified in all the essential aspects of its life, its political machinery, its spiritual aspiration, its trade and finance, its script and language, and yet infinite in the diversity of the national characteristics of its federated units.

It represents the consummation of human evolution—an evolution that has had its earliest beginnings in the birth of family life, its subsequent development in the achievement of tribal solidarity, leading in turn to the constitution of the city-state, and expanding later into the institution of independent and sovereign nations.

The principle of the Oneness of Mankind, as proclaimed by Bahá'u'lláh, carries with it no more and no less than a solemn assertion that attainment to this final stage in this stupendous evolution is not only necessary but inevitable, that its realization is fast approaching, and that nothing short of a power that is born of God can succeed in establishing it. . . .

Who knows that for so exalted a conception to

take shape a suffering more intense than any it has yet experienced will have to be inflicted upon humanity? Could anything less than the fire of a civil war with all its violence and vicissitudes—a war that nearly rent the great American Republic—have welded the states, not only into a Union of independent units, but into a Nation, in spite of all the ethnic differences that characterized its component parts? That so fundamental a revolution, involving such far-reaching changes in the structure of society, can be achieved through the ordinary processes of diplomacy and education seems highly improbable. We have but to turn our gaze to humanity's blood-stained history to realize that nothing short of intense mental as well as physical agony has been able to precipitate those epoch-making changes that constitute the greatest landmarks in the history of human civilization.

Great and far-reaching as have been those changes in the past, they cannot appear, when viewed in their proper perspective, except as subsidiary adjustments preluding that transformation of unparalleled majesty and scope which humanity is in this age bound to undergo. That the forces of a world catastrophe can alone precipitate such a new phase of human thought is, alas, becoming increasingly apparent. That nothing short of the fire of a severe ordeal, unparalleled in its intensity, can fuse and weld the discordant entities that constitute the elements of present-day civilization, into the integral components of the world commonwealth of the future, is a truth which future events will increasingly demonstrate.

The prophetic voice of Bahá'u'lláh warning, in the concluding passages of *The Hidden Words,* the peoples of the world that an unforeseen calamity is following them and that grievous retribution awaiteth them throws indeed a lurid light upon the immediate fortunes of sorrowing humanity. Nothing but a fiery ordeal, out of which humanity will emerge, chastened and prepared, can succeed in implanting that sense of responsibility which the leaders of a new-born age must arise to shoulder.

I would again direct your attention to those ominous words of Bahá'u'lláh which I have already quoted: *"And when the appointed hour is come, there shall suddenly appear that which shall cause the limbs of mankind to quake."* ...

One word more in conclusion. The proclamation of the Oneness of Mankind—the head corner-stone of Bahá'u'lláh's all-embracing dominion—can under no circumstances be compared with such expressions of pious hope as have been uttered in the past. His is not merely a call which He raised, alone and unaided, in the face of the relentless and combined opposition of two of the most powerful Oriental potentates of His day—while Himself an exile and prisoner in their hands. It implies at once a warning and a promise—a warning that in it lies the sole means for the salvation of a greatly suffering world, a promise that its realization is at hand.

Uttered at a time when its possibility had not yet been seriously envisaged in any part of the world, it has, by virtue of that celestial potency which the Spirit of Bahá'u'lláh has breathed into it, come at last to be regarded, by an increasing number of thoughtful men, not only as an approaching possibility, but as the necessary outcome of the forces now operating in the world.

Surely the world, contracted and transformed into a single highly complex organism by the marvellous progress achieved in the realm of physical science, by the world-wide expansion of commerce and industry, and struggling, under the pressure of world economic forces, amidst the pitfalls of a materialistic civilization, stands in dire need of a restatement of the Truth underlying all the Revelations of the past in a language suited to its essential requirements. And what voice other than that of Bahá'u'lláh—the Mouthpiece of God for this age—is capable of effecting a transformation of society as radical as that which He has already accomplished in the hearts of those men and women, so diversified and seemingly irreconcilable, who constitute the body of His declared followers throughout the world?

That such a mighty conception is fast budding out

in the minds of men, that voices are being raised in its support, that its salient features must fast crystallize in the consciousness of those who are in authority, few indeed can doubt. That its modest beginnings have already taken shape in the world-wide Administration with which the adherents of the Faith of Bahá'u'lláh stand associated only those whose hearts are tainted by prejudice can fail to perceive. . . .

III

A Pattern for Future Society

Few will fail to recognize that the Spirit breathed by
Bahá'u'lláh upon the world, and which is manifesting
itself with varying degrees of intensity through the
efforts consciously displayed by His avowed supporters and indirectly through certain humanitarian
organizations, can never permeate and exercise an
abiding influence upon mankind unless and until it
incarnates itself in a visible Order, which would bear
His name, wholly identify itself with His principles,
and function in conformity with His laws. That
Bahá'u'lláh in His Book of *Aqdas,* and later 'Abdu'l-
Bahá in His Will—a document which confirms,
supplements, and correlates the provisions of the
Aqdas—have set forth in their entirety those essential
elements for the constitution of the world Bahá'í
Commonwealth, no one who has read them will deny.
According to these divinely-ordained administrative
principles, the Dispensation of Bahá'u'lláh—the Ark
of human salvation—must needs be modelled. From

them, all future blessings must flow, and upon them its inviolable authority must ultimately rest.

For Bahá'u'lláh, we should readily recognize, has not only imbued mankind with a new and regenerating Spirit. He has not merely enunciated certain universal principles, or propounded a particular philosophy, however potent, sound and universal these may be. In addition to these He, as well as 'Abdu'l-Bahá after Him, has, unlike the Dispensations of the past, clearly and specifically laid down a set of Laws, established definite institutions, and provided for the essentials of a Divine Economy. These are destined to be a pattern for future society, a supreme instrument for the establishment of the Most Great Peace, and the one agency for the unification of the world, and the proclamation of the reign of righteousness and justice upon the earth. . . .

Leaders of religion, exponents of political theories, governors of human institutions, who at present are witnessing with perplexity and dismay the bankruptcy of their ideas, and the disintegration of their handiwork, would do well to turn their gaze to the Revelation of Bahá'u'lláh, and to meditate upon the World Order which, lying enshrined in His teachings, is slowly and imperceptibly rising amid the welter and chaos of present-day civilization. They need have no doubt or anxiety regarding the nature, the origin or validity of the institutions which the adherents of the

37

Faith are building up throughout the world. For these lie embedded in the teachings themselves, unadulterated and unobscured by unwarrantable inferences, or unauthorized interpretations of His Word....

The onrushing forces so miraculously released through the agency of two independent and swiftly successive Manifestations are now under our very eyes and through the care of the chosen stewards of a far-flung Faith being gradually mustered and disciplined. They are slowly crystallizing into institutions that will come to be regarded as the hall-mark and glory of the age we are called upon to establish and by our deeds immortalize....

It would be utterly misleading to attempt a comparison between this unique, this divinely-conceived Order and any of the diverse systems which the minds of men, at various periods of their history, have contrived for the government of human institutions. Such an attempt would in itself betray a lack of complete appreciation of the excellence of the handiwork of its great Author. How could it be otherwise when we remember that this Order constitutes the very pattern of that divine civilization which the almighty Law of Bahá'u'lláh is designed to establish upon earth? The divers and ever-shifting systems of human polity, whether past or present, whether originating in the East or in the West, offer no adequate criterion wherewith to estimate the potency of its hidden virtues or to appraise the solidity of its foundations.

The Bahá'í Commonwealth of the future, of which this vast Administrative Order is the sole framework, is, both in theory and practice, not only unique in the entire history of political institutions, but can find no parallel in the annals of any of the world's recognized religious systems. No form of democratic government; no system of autocracy or of dictatorship, whether monarchical or republican; no intermediary scheme of a purely aristocratic order; nor even any of the recognized types of theocracy, whether it be the Hebrew Commonwealth, or the various Christian ecclesiastical organizations, or the Imamate or the Caliphate in Islám—none of these can be identified or be said to conform with the Administrative Order which the master-hand of its perfect Architect has fashioned.

This new-born Administrative Order incorporates within its structure certain elements which are to be found in each of the three recognized forms of secular government, without being in any sense a mere replica of any one of them, and without introducing within its machinery any of the objectionable features which they inherently possess. It blends and harmonizes, as no government fashioned by mortal hands has as yet accomplished, the salutary truths which each of these systems undoubtedly contains without vitiating the integrity of those God-given verities on which it is ultimately founded.

The Administrative Order of the Faith of Bahá'u'lláh must in no wise be regarded as purely democratic in character inasmuch as the basic assumption which requires all democracies to depend fundamentally upon getting their mandate from the people is altogether lacking in this Dispensation. In the conduct of the administrative affairs of the Faith, in the enactment of the legislation necessary to supplement the laws of the *Kitáb-i-Aqdas,* the members of the Universal House of Justice, it should be borne in mind, are not, as Bahá'u'lláh's utterances clearly imply, responsible to those whom they represent, nor are they allowed to be governed by the feelings, the general opinion, and even the convictions of the mass of the faithful, or of those who directly elect them. They are to follow, in a prayerful attitude, the dictates and promptings of their conscience. They may, indeed they must, acquaint themselves with the conditions prevailing among the community, must weigh dispassionately in their minds the merits of any case presented for their consideration, but must reserve for themselves the right of an unfettered decision. "*God will verily inspire them with whatsoever He willeth,*" is Bahá'u'lláh's incontrovertible assurance. They, and not the body of those who either directly or indirectly elect them, have thus been made the recipients of the divine guidance which is at once the life-blood and ultimate safeguard of this Revelation. . . .

Nor can the Bahá'í Administrative Order be dismissed as a hard and rigid system of unmitigated autocracy or as an idle imitation of any form of absolutistic ecclesiastical government, whether it be the Papacy, the Imamate or any other similar institution, for the obvious reason that upon the international elected representatives of the followers of Bahá'u'lláh has been conferred the exclusive right of legislating on matters not expressly revealed in the Bahá'í writings. Neither the Guardian of the Faith nor any institution apart from the International House of Justice can ever usurp this vital and essential power or encroach upon that sacred right. The abolition of professional priesthood with its accompanying sacraments of baptism, of communion and of confession of sins, the laws requiring the election by universal suffrage of all local, national, and international Houses of Justice, the total absence of episcopal authority with its attendant privileges, corruptions and bureaucratic tendencies, are further evidences of the non-autocratic character of the Bahá'í Administrative Order and of its inclination to democratic methods in the administration of its affairs.

Nor is this Order identified with the name of

Bahá'u'lláh to be confused with any system of purely aristocratic government in view of the fact that it upholds, on the one hand, the hereditary principle and entrusts the Guardian of the Faith with the obligation of interpreting its teachings, and provides, on the other, for the free and direct election from among the mass of the faithful of the body that constitutes its highest legislative organ.

Whereas this Administrative Order cannot be said to have been modelled after any of these recognized systems of government, it nevertheless embodies, reconciles and assimilates within its framework such wholesome elements as are to be found in each one of them. The hereditary authority which the Guardian is called upon to exercise, the vital and essential functions which the Universal House of Justice discharges, the specific provisions requiring its democratic election by the representatives of the faithful— these combine to demonstrate the truth that this divinely revealed Order, which can never be identified with any of the standard types of government referred to by Aristotle in his works, embodies and blends with the spiritual verities on which it is based the beneficent elements which are to be found in each one of them. The admitted evils inherent in each of these systems being rigidly and permanently excluded, this unique Order, however long it may endure and however extensive its ramifications, cannot ever degenerate into any form of despotism, of oligarchy, or of demagogy which must sooner or later corrupt the machinery of all man-made and essentially defective political institutions. . . .

Significant as are the origins of this mighty administrative structure, and however unique its features, the happenings that may be said to have heralded its birth and signalized the initial stage of its evolution seem no less remarkable. How striking, how edifying the contrast between the process of slow and steady consolidation that characterizes the growth of its infant strength and the devastating onrush of the forces of disintegration that are assailing the outworn institutions, both religious and secular, of present-day society!

The vitality which the organic institutions of this great, this ever-expanding Order so strongly exhibit; the obstacles which the high courage, the undaunted resolution of its administrators have already surmounted; the fire of an unquenchable enthusiasm that glows with undiminished fervour in the hearts of its itinerant teachers; the heights of self-sacrifice which its champion-builders are now attaining; the breadth of vision, the confident hope, the creative joy, the inward peace, the uncompromising integrity, the exemplary discipline, the unyielding unity and solidarity which its stalwart defenders manifest; the degree to which its moving Spirit has shown itself capable of assimilating the diversified elements within its pale, of cleansing them of all forms of prejudice and of fusing them with its own structure—these are evidences of a power which a disillusioned and sadly shaken society can ill afford to ignore.

Compare these splendid manifestations of the spirit animating this vibrant body of the Faith of Bahá'u'lláh with the cries and agony, the follies and vanities, the bitterness and prejudices, the wickedness and divisions of an ailing and chaotic world. Witness the fear that torments its leaders and paralyzes the action of its blind and bewildered statesmen. How fierce the hatreds, how false the ambitions, how petty the pursuits, how deep-rooted the suspicions of its peoples! How disquieting the lawlessness, the corruption, the unbelief that are eating into the vitals of a tottering civilization!

Might not this process of steady deterioration which is insidiously invading so many departments of human activity and thought be regarded as a necessary accompaniment to the rise of this almighty Arm of Bahá'u'lláh? Might we not look upon the momentous happenings which . . . have so deeply agitated every continent of the earth, as ominous signs simultaneously proclaiming the agonies of a disintegrating civilization and the birthpangs of that World Order—that Ark of human salvation—that must needs arise upon its ruins?

IV

World Commonwealth

The contrast between the accumulating evidences of steady consolidation that accompany the rise of the Administrative Order of the Faith of God, and the forces of disintegration which batter at the fabric of a travailing society, is as clear as it is arresting. Both within and outside the Bahá'í world the signs and tokens which, in a mysterious manner, are heralding the birth of that World Order, the establishment of which must signalize the Golden Age of the Cause of God, are growing and multiplying day by day. No fair-minded observer can any longer fail to discern them. He cannot be misled by the painful slowness characterizing the unfoldment of the civilization which the followers of Bahá'u'lláh are labouring to establish. Nor can he be deluded by the ephemeral manifestations of returning prosperity which at times appear to be capable of checking the disruptive influence of the chronic ills afflicting the institutions of a decaying age. The signs of the times are too numerous and compelling to allow him to mistake their character or to belittle their significance. He can, if he be fair in his judgement, recognize in the chain of events which proclaim on the one hand the irresistible march of the institutions directly associated with the Revelation of Bahá'u'lláh and foreshadow on the other the downfall of those powers and principalities that have either ignored or opposed it—he can recognize in them all evidences of the operation of God's all-pervasive Will, the shaping of His perfectly ordered and world-embracing Plan.

"*Soon,*" Bahá'u'lláh's own words proclaim it, "*will the present day Order be rolled up, and a new one spread out in its stead. Verily, thy Lord speaketh the truth and is the Knower of things unseen.*" "*By Myself,*" He solemnly asserts, "*the day is approaching when We will have rolled up the world and all that is therein, and spread out a new Order in its stead. He, verily, is powerful over all things.*" "*The world's equilibrium,*" He explains, "*hath been upset through the vibrating influence of this Most Great, this new World Order. Mankind's ordered life hath been revolutionized through the agency of this unique, this wondrous System, the like of which mortal eyes have never witnessed.*" "*The signs of impending convulsions and chaos,*" He warns the peoples of the world, "*can now be discerned, inasmuch as the prevailing Order appeareth to be lamentably defective.*" . . .

No machinery falling short of the standard inculcated by the Bahá'í Revelation, and at variance with the sublime pattern ordained in His teachings, which the collective efforts of mankind may yet devise can ever hope to achieve anything above or beyond that *"Lesser Peace"* to which the Author of our Faith has Himself alluded in His writings. *"Now that ye have refused the Most Great Peace,"* He, admonishing the kings and rulers of the earth, has written, *"hold ye fast unto this the Lesser Peace, that haply ye may in some degree better your own condition and that of your dependents."* Expatiating on this Lesser Peace, He thus addresses in that same Tablet the rulers of the earth: *"Be reconciled among yourselves, that ye may need no more armaments save in a measure to safeguard your territories and dominions . . . Be united, O kings of the earth, for thereby will the tempest of discord be stilled amongst you, and your peoples find rest, if ye be of them that comprehend. Should any one among you take up arms against another, rise ye all against him, for this is naught but manifest justice."*

The Most Great Peace, on the other hand, as conceived by Bahá'u'lláh—a peace that must inevitably follow as the practical consequence of the spiritualization of the world and the fusion of all its races, creeds, classes and nations—can rest on no other basis, and can be preserved through no other agency, except the divinely appointed ordinances that are implicit in the World Order that stands associated with His holy

47

name. In His Tablet, revealed almost seventy[1] years ago to Queen Victoria, Bahá'u'lláh, alluding to this Most Great Peace, has declared: "*That which the Lord hath ordained as the sovereign remedy and mightiest instrument for the healing of all the world is the union of all its peoples in one universal Cause, one common Faith. This can in no wise be achieved except through the power of a skilled, an all-powerful and inspired Physician. This, verily, is the truth, and all else naught but error*" . . . "*It beseemeth all men in this Day,*" He, in another Tablet, asserts, "*to take firm hold on the Most Great Name, and to establish the unity of all mankind. There is no place to flee to, no refuge that any one can seek, except Him.*"

The Revelation of Bahá'u'lláh, whose supreme mission is none other but the achievement of this organic and spiritual unity of the whole body of nations, should, if we be faithful to its implications, be regarded as signalizing through its advent the *coming of age of the entire human race*. It should be viewed not merely as yet another spiritual revival in the ever-changing fortunes of mankind, not only as a further stage in a chain of progressive Revelations, nor even as the culmination of one of a series of recurrent prophetic cycles, but rather as marking the last and highest stage in the stupendous evolution of man's collective life on this planet. The emergence of a world community, the consciousness of world citizen-

[1] Now more than a hundred.

48

ship, the founding of a world civilization and culture —all of which must synchronize with the initial stages in the unfoldment of the Golden Age of the Bahá'í Era—should, by their very nature, be regarded, as far as this planetary life is concerned, as the furthermost limits in the organization of human society, though man, as an individual, will, nay must indeed as a result of such a consummation, continue indefinitely to progress and develop.

That mystic, all-pervasive, yet indefinable change, which we associate with the stage of maturity inevitable in the life of the individual and the development of the fruit must, if we would correctly apprehend the utterances of Bahá'u'lláh, have its counterpart in the evolution of the organization of human society. A similar stage must sooner or later be attained in the collective life of mankind, producing an even more striking phenomenon in world relations, and endowing the whole human race with such potentialities of well-being as shall provide, throughout the succeeding ages, the chief incentive required for the eventual fulfilment of its high destiny. . . .

Only those who are willing to associate the Revelation proclaimed by Bahá'u'lláh with the consummation of so stupendous an evolution in the collective life of the whole human race can grasp the significance of the words which He, while alluding to the glories of this promised Day and to the duration of

49

the Bahá'í Era, has deemed fit to utter. *"This is the King of Days,"* He exclaims, *"the Day that hath seen the coming of the Best-Beloved, Him Who, through all eternity, hath been acclaimed the Desire of the World."* *"The Scriptures of past Dispensations,"* He further asserts, *"celebrate the great jubilee that must needs greet this most great Day of God. Well is it with him that hath lived to see this Day and hath recognized its station."* . . .

Though the Revelation of Bahá'u'lláh has been delivered, the World Order which such a Revelation must needs beget is as yet unborn. Though the Heroic Age of His Faith is passed, the creative energies which that Age has released have not as yet crystallized into that world society which, in the fullness of time, is to mirror forth the brightness of His glory. Though the framework of His Administrative Order has been erected, and the Formative Period of the Bahá'í Era has begun, yet the promised Kingdom into which the seed of His institutions must ripen remains as yet uninaugurated. Though His Voice has been raised, and the ensigns of His Faith have been lifted up in no less than forty countries[1] of both the East and the West, yet the wholeness of the human race is as yet unrecognized, its unity unproclaimed, and the standard of its Most Great Peace unhoisted. . . .

For the revelation of so great a favour a period of

[1] Written in 1936, since when the number has increased to 335, comprising 152 independent states and 183 territories.

intense turmoil and widespread suffering would seem to be indispensable. Resplendent as has been the Age that has witnessed the inception of the Mission with which Bahá'u'lláh has been entrusted, the interval which must elapse ere that Age yields its choicest fruit must, it is becoming increasingly apparent, be overshadowed by such moral and social gloom as can alone prepare an unrepentant humanity for the prize she is destined to inherit.

Into such a period we are now steadily and irresistibly moving. Amidst the shadows which are increasingly gathering about us we can faintly discern the glimmerings of Bahá'u'lláh's unearthly sovereignty appearing fitfully on the horizon of history. To us, the "generation of the half-light," living at a time which may be designated as the period of the incubation of the World Commonwealth envisaged by Bahá'u'lláh, has been assigned a task whose high privilege we can never sufficiently appreciate, and the arduousness of which we can as yet but dimly recognize. We may well believe, we who are called upon to experience the operation of the dark forces destined to unloose a flood of agonizing afflictions, that the darkest hour that must precede the dawn of the Golden Age of our Faith has not yet struck. Deep as is the gloom that already encircles the world, the afflictive ordeals which that world is to suffer are still in preparation, nor can their blackness be as yet imagined. We stand on the threshold of an age whose convulsions proclaim alike the death-pangs of the old order and the birth-pangs of the new. Through the generating influence of the Faith announced by Bahá'u'lláh this New World Order may be said to have been conceived. We can, at the present moment, experience its stirrings in the womb of a travailing age—an age waiting for the appointed hour at which it can cast its burden and yield its fairest fruit.

"*The whole earth,*" writes Bahá'u'lláh, "*is now in a state of pregnancy. The day is approaching when it will have yielded its noblest fruits, when from it will have sprung forth the loftiest trees, the most enchanting blossoms, the most heavenly blessings. . . .*"

"*The Call of God,*" 'Abdu'l-Bahá has written, "*when raised, breathed a new life into the body of mankind, and infused a new spirit into the whole creation. It is for this reason that the world hath been moved to its depths, and the hearts and consciences of men been quickened. Erelong the evidences of this regeneration will be revealed, and the fast asleep will be awakened.*" . . .

Unification of the whole of mankind is the hall-mark of the stage which human society is now approaching. Unity of family, of tribe, of city-state, and nation have been successively attempted and fully established. World unity is the goal towards which a harassed humanity is striving. Nation-building has come to an end. The anarchy inherent in state sovereignty is moving towards a climax. A world, growing to maturity, must abandon this fetish, recognize the oneness and wholeness of human relationships, and establish once for all the machinery that can best incarnate this fundamental principle of its life.

"*A new life,*" Bahá'u'lláh proclaims, "*is, in this age, stirring within all the peoples of the earth; and yet none hath discovered its cause, or perceived its motive.*" "*O ye children of men,*" He thus addresses His generation, "*the fundamental purpose animating the Faith of God and His Religion is to safeguard the interests and promote the unity of the human race . . . This is the straight path, the fixed and immovable foundation. Whatsoever is raised on this foundation, the changes and chances of the world can never impair its strength, nor will the revolution of countless centuries undermine its structure.*" "*The well-being of mankind,*" He declares, "*its peace and security are unattainable unless and until its unity is firmly established.*" "*So powerful is the light of unity,*" is His further testimony, "*that it can illuminate the whole earth. The one true God, He Who knoweth all things, Himself testifieth to the truth of these words . . . This goal excelleth every other goal, and this aspiration is the monarch of all aspirations.*" "*He Who is your Lord, the All-Merciful,*" He, moreover, has written, "*cherisheth in His heart the desire of beholding the entire human race as one soul and one body. Haste ye to win your share of God's good grace and mercy in this Day that eclipseth all other created days.*"

The unity of the human race, as envisaged by Bahá'u'lláh, implies the establishment of a world commonwealth in which all nations, races, creeds and classes are closely and permanently united, and in which the autonomy of its state members and the personal freedom and initiative of the individuals that compose them are definitely and completely safeguarded. This commonwealth must, as far as we can visualize it, consist of a world legislature, whose members will, as the trustees of the whole of mankind, ultimately control the entire resources of all the component nations, and will enact such laws as shall be required to regulate the life, satisfy the needs and adjust the relationships of all races and peoples. A world executive, backed by an international Force, will carry out the decisions arrived at, and apply the laws enacted by, this world legislature, and will safeguard the organic unity of the whole commonwealth. A world tribunal will adjudicate and deliver its compulsory and final verdict in all and any disputes that may arise between the various elements constituting this universal system. A mechanism of world intercommunication will be devised, embracing the whole planet, freed from national hindrances and restrictions, and functioning with marvellous swiftness and perfect regularity. A world metropolis will act as the nerve centre of a world civilization, the focus towards which the unifying forces of life will converge and

54

from which its energizing influences will radiate. A world language will either be invented or chosen from among the existing languages and will be taught in the schools of all the federated nations as an auxiliary to their mother tongue. A world script, a world literature, a uniform and universal system of currency, of weights and measures, will simplify and facilitate intercourse and understanding among the nations and races of mankind. In such a world society, science and religion, the two most potent forces in human life, will be reconciled, will cooperate, and will harmoniously develop. The press will, under such a system, while giving full scope to the expression of the diversified views and convictions of mankind, cease to be mischievously manipulated by vested interests, whether private or public, and will be liberated from the influence of contending governments and peoples. The economic resources of the world will be organized, its sources of raw materials will be tapped and fully utilized, its markets will be coordinated and developed, and the distribution of its products will be equitably regulated.

National rivalries, hatreds, and intrigues will cease, and racial animosity and prejudice will be replaced by racial amity, understanding and cooperation. The causes of religious strife will be permanently removed, economic barriers and restrictions will be completely abolished, and the inordinate distinction between classes will be obliterated. Destitution on the one hand, and gross accumulation of ownership on the other, will disappear. The enormous energy dissipated and wasted on war, whether economic or political, will be consecrated to such ends as will extend the range of human inventions and technical development, to the increase of the productivity of mankind, to the extermination of disease, to the extension of scientific research, to the raising of the standard of physical health, to the sharpening and refinement of the human brain, to the exploitation of the unused and unsuspected resources of the planet, to the prolongation of human life, and to the furtherance of any other agency that can stimulate the intellectual, the moral, and spiritual life of the entire human race.

A world federal system, ruling the whole earth and exercising unchallengeable authority over its unimaginably vast resources, blending and embodying the ideals of both the East and the West, liberated from the curse of war and its miseries, and bent on the exploitation of all the available sources of energy on the surface of the planet, a system in which Force is made the servant of Justice, whose life is sustained by its universal recognition of one God and by its allegiance to one common Revelation—such is the goal towards which humanity, impelled by the unifying forces of life, is moving.

V

The Destiny of Mankind

As we gaze in retrospect beyond the immediate past, and survey, in however cursory a manner, the vicissitudes afflicting an increasingly tormented society, and recall the strains and stresses to which the fabric of a dying Order has been increasingly subjected, we cannot but marvel at the sharp contrast presented, on the one hand, by the accumulated evidences of the orderly unfoldment, and the uninterrupted multiplication of the agencies, of an Administrative Order designed to be the harbinger of a world civilization, and, on the other, by the ominous manifestations of acute political conflict, of social unrest, of racial animosity, of class antagonism, of immorality and of irreligion, proclaiming, in no uncertain terms, the corruption and obsolescence of the institutions of a bankrupt Order....

"*The winds of despair,*" writes Bahá'u'lláh, as He

surveys the immediate destinies of mankind, *"are, alas, blowing from every direction, and the strife that divides and afflicts the human race is daily increasing. . . ."* *"Such shall be its plight,"* He, in another connection, has declared, *"that to disclose it now would not be meet and seemly."* *"These fruitless strifes,"* He, on the other hand, contemplating the future of mankind, has emphatically prophesied, in the course of His memorable interview with the Persian orientalist, Edward G. Browne, *"these ruinous wars shall pass away, and the 'Most Great Peace' shall come. . . . These strifes and this bloodshed and discord must cease, and all men be as one kindred and one family."* . . .

"All nations and kindreds," 'Abdu'l-Bahá likewise has written, *" . . . will become a single nation. Religious and sectarian antagonism, the hostility of races and peoples, and differences among nations, will be eliminated. All men will adhere to one religion, will have one common faith, will be blended into one race, and become a single people. All will dwell in one common fatherland, which is the planet itself."*

What we witness at the present time, during "this gravest crisis in the history of civilization," recalling such times in which "religions have perished and are born," is the adolescent stage in the slow and painful evolution of humanity, preparatory to the attainment of the stage of manhood, the stage of maturity, the promise of which is embedded in the teachings, and enshrined in the prophecies, of Bahá'u'lláh. The tumult of this age of transition is characteristic of the impetuosity and irrational instincts of youth, its follies, its prodigality, its pride, its self-assurance, its rebelliousness, and contempt of discipline.

The ages of its infancy and childhood are past, never again to return, while the Great Age, the consummation of all ages, which must signalize the coming of age of the entire human race, is yet to come. The convulsions of this transitional and most turbulent period in the annals of humanity are the essential prerequisites, and herald the inevitable approach, of that Age of Ages, *"the time of the end,"* in which the folly and tumult of strife that has, since the dawn of history, blackened the annals of mankind, will have been finally transmuted into the wisdom and the tranquillity of an undisturbed, a universal, and lasting peace, in which the discord and separation of the children of men will have given way to the worldwide reconciliation, and the complete unification of the divers elements that constitute human society.

This will indeed be the fitting climax of that process of integration which, starting with the family, the smallest unit in the scale of human organization, must, after having called successively into being the tribe, the city-state and the nation, continue to operate until it culminates in the unification of the whole world, the final object and the crowning glory of human evolution on this planet. It is this stage which humanity, willingly or unwillingly, is resistlessly approaching. It is for this stage that this vast, this fiery ordeal which humanity is experiencing is mysteriously paving the way. It is with this stage that the fortunes and the purpose of the Faith of Bahá'u'lláh are indissolubly linked. It is the creative energies which His Revelation has released . . . that have instilled into humanity the capacity to attain this final stage in its organic and collective evolution. It is with the Golden Age of His Dispensation that the consummation of this process will be for ever associated. It is the structure of His New World Order, now stirring in the womb of the administrative institutions He Himself has created, that will serve both as a pattern and a nucleus of that world commonwealth which is the sure, the inevitable destiny of the peoples and nations of the earth.

Just as the organic evolution of mankind has been slow and gradual, and involved successively the unification of the family, the tribe, the city-state, and the nation, so has the light vouchsafed by the Revelation of God, at various stages in the evolution of religion, and reflected in the successive Dispensations of the past, been slow and progressive. Indeed the measure of Divine Revelation, in every age, has been adapted to, and commensurate with, the degree of social progress achieved in that age by a constantly-evolving humanity.

"*It hath been decreed by Us,*" explains Bahá'u'lláh, "*that the Word of God, and all the potentialities thereof, shall be manifested unto men in strict conformity with such conditions as have been fore-ordained by Him Who is the All-Knowing, the All-Wise. . . . Should the Word be allowed to release suddenly all the energies latent within it, no man could sustain the weight of so mighty a Revelation.*" "*All created things,*" 'Abdu'l-Bahá elucidating this truth, has affirmed, "*have their degree or stage of maturity. The period of maturity in the life of a tree is the time of its fruit-bearing. . . . The animal attains a stage of full growth and completeness, and in the human kingdom man reaches his maturity when the light of his intelligence attains its greatest power and development. . . . Similarly there are periods and stages in the collective life of humanity. At one time it was passing through its stage of childhood, at another its period of youth, but now it has entered its long-predicted phase of maturity, the evidences of which are everywhere apparent. . . . That which was applicable to human needs during the early history of the race can neither meet nor satisfy the demands of this day, this period of newness and consummation. Humanity has emerged from its former state of limitation and preliminary training. Man must now become imbued with new virtues and powers, new moral standards, new capacities. New bounties, perfect bestowals, are awaiting and already descending upon him. The gifts and blessings of the period of youth, although timely and sufficient during the adolescence of mankind, are now incapable of meeting the requirements of its maturity."* . . .

This is the stage which the world is now approaching, the stage of world unity, which, as 'Abdu'l-Bahá assures us, will, in this century, be securely established. *"The Tongue of Grandeur,"* Bahá'u'lláh Himself affirms, *"hath . . . in the Day of His Manifestation proclaimed: 'It is not his to boast who loveth his country, but it is his who loveth the world.'"* *"Through the power,"* He adds, *"released by these exalted words He hath lent a fresh impulse, and set a new direction, to the birds of men's hearts, and hath obliterated every trace of restriction and limitation from God's Holy Book."*

A word of warning should, however, be uttered in this connection. The love of one's country, instilled and stressed by the teaching of Islám, as *"an element of the Faith of God"* has not, through this declaration, this clarion-call of Bahá'u'lláh, been either condemned or disparaged. It should not, indeed it cannot, be construed as a repudiation, or regarded in the light of a censure pronounced against, a sane and intelligent patriotism, nor does it seek to undermine the allegiance and loyalty of any individual to his country, nor does it conflict with the legitimate aspirations, rights, and duties of any individual state or nation. All it does imply and proclaim is the insufficiency of patriotism, in view of the fundamental changes effected in the economic life of society and the interdependence of

62

the nations, and as the consequence of the contraction of the world, through the revolution in the means of transportation and communication—conditions that did not and could not exist either in the days of Jesus Christ or of Muḥammad. It calls for a wider loyalty, which should not, and indeed does not, conflict with lesser loyalties. It instills a love which, in view of its scope, must include and not exclude the love of one's own country. It lays, through this loyalty which it inspires, and this love which it infuses, the only foundation on which the concept of world citizenship can thrive, and the structure of world unification can rest. It does insist, however, on the subordination of national considerations and particularistic interests to the imperative and paramount claims of humanity as a whole, inasmuch as in a world of interdependent nations and peoples the advantage of the part is best to be reached by the advantage of the whole.

The world is, in truth, moving on towards its destiny. The interdependence of the peoples and nations of the earth, whatever the leaders of the divisive forces of the world may say or do, is already an accomplished fact. Its unity in the economic sphere is now understood and recognized. The welfare of the part means the welfare of the whole, and the distress of the part brings distress to the whole. The Revelation of Bahá'u'lláh has, in His own words, *"lent a fresh impulse and set a new direction"* to this vast process now operating in the world. The fires lit by this great ordeal are the consequences of men's failure to recognize it. They are, moreover, hastening its consummation. Adversity, prolonged, world-wide, afflictive, allied to chaos and universal destruction, must needs convulse the nations, stir the conscience of the world, disillusion the masses, precipitate a radical change in the very conception of society, and coalesce ultimately the disjointed, the bleeding limbs of mankind into one body, single, organically united, and indivisible.

To the general character, the implications and features of this world commonwealth, destined to emerge, sooner or later, out of the carnage, agony, and havoc of this great world convulsion, I have already referred in my previous communications. Suffice it to say that this consummation will, by its very nature, be a gradual process, and must, as Bahá'u'lláh has Himself anticipated, lead at first to the establishment of that Lesser Peace which the nations of the earth, as yet unconscious of His Revelation and yet unwittingly enforcing the general principles which He has enunciated, will themselves establish. This momentous and historic step, involving the reconstruction of mankind, as the result of the universal recognition of its oneness and wholeness, will bring in its wake the spiritualization of the masses, consequent to the recognition of the character, and the acknowledgment of the claims, of the Faith of Bahá'-u'lláh—the essential condition to that ultimate fusion of all races, creeds, classes, and nations which must signalize the emergence of His New World Order.

Then will the coming of age of the entire human race be proclaimed and celebrated by all the peoples and nations of the earth. Then will the banner of the Most Great Peace be hoisted. Then will the world-wide sovereignty of Bahá'u'lláh—the Establisher of the Kingdom of the Father foretold by the Son, and anticipated by the Prophets of God before Him and after Him—be recognized, acclaimed, and firmly established. Then will a world civilization be born, flourish, and perpetuate itself, a civilization with a fullness of life such as the world has never seen nor can as yet conceive. Then will the Everlasting Covenant be fulfilled in its completeness. Then will the promise enshrined in all the Books of God be redeemed, and all the prophecies uttered by the Prophets of old come to pass, and the vision of seers and poets be realized. Then will the planet, galvanized through the universal belief of its dwellers in one God, and their allegiance to one common Revelation, mirror, within the limitations imposed upon it, the effulgent glories of the sovereignty of Bahá'u'lláh, shining in the plenitude of its splendour in the Abhá Paradise, and be made the footstool of His Throne on high, and acclaimed as the earthly heaven, capable of fulfilling that ineffable destiny fixed for it, from time immemorial, by the love and wisdom of its Creator.

Not ours, puny mortals that we are, to attempt, at so critical a stage in the long and chequered history of mankind, to arrive at a precise and satisfactory understanding of the steps which must successively lead a bleeding humanity, wretchedly oblivious of its God, and careless of Bahá'u'lláh, from its calvary to its ultimate resurrection. Not ours, the living witnesses of the all-subduing potency of His Faith, to question, for a moment, and however dark the misery that enshrouds the world, the ability of Bahá'u'lláh to forge, with the hammer of His will, and through the fire of tribulation, upon the anvil of this travailing age, and in the particular shape His mind has envisioned, these scattered and mutually destructive fragments into which a perverse world has fallen, into one single unit, solid and indivisible, able to execute His design for the children of men.

Ours rather the duty, however confused the scene, however dismal the present outlook, however circumscribed the resources we dispose of, to labour serenely, confidently and unremittingly to lend our share of assistance, in whichever way circumstances may enable us, to the operation of the forces which, as marshalled and directed by Bahá'u'lláh, are leading humanity out of the valley of misery and shame to the loftiest summits of power and glory.

References

The published works of Shoghi Effendi, from which the extracts in this book have been selected, are:

	Reference
The World Order of Bahá'u'lláh—Further Considerations (March, 1930)	WOB-FC
The Goal of a New World Order (November, 1931)	GNWO
The Dispensation of Bahá'u'lláh (February, 1934)	DB
The Unfoldment of World Civilization (March, 1936)	UWC
The Promised Day is Come (March, 1941)	PDC
God Passes By (1944)	GPB
Messages to the Bahá'í World 1950–1957 (1958)	MBW

The first four titles, although published separately, were, in 1938, included in a compilation of Shoghi Effendi's writings published under the title, *The World Order of Bahá'u'lláh*. Since this volume is now the more generally available source of these four letters, extracts from them have been referred to that volume, e.g. *GNWO-WOB, 33–48*. The remaining works quoted are published individually.

The references given are to the editions of the Bahá'í Publishing Trust of the United States.

page line

1   1   The Introduction consists of extracts from a statement prepared by Shoghi Effendi for the United Nations Special Committee on Palestine, July 1947.

REFERENCES

page	*line*	
45	1	"The contrast between" to "'*appeareth to be lamentably defective.*'" (*UWC–WOB, 161–162*)
46	28	"No machinery falling short" to "fulfillment of its high destiny." (*UWC–WOB*, 162–164)
49	23	"Only those who are willing" to "'*recognized its station.*'" (*UWC–WOB*, 166–167)
50	9	"Though the Revelation of Bahá'u'lláh" to "Most Great Peace unhoisted." (*UWC–WOB*, 168)
50	26	"For the revelation" to "'*most heavenly blessings.*'" (*UWC–WOB*, 168–169)
52	15	"'*The Call of God,*'" to "'*fast asleep will be awakened.*'" (*UWC–WOB*, 169)
52	22	"Unification of the whole of mankind" to "unifying forces of life, is moving." (*UWC–WOB*, 202–204)
57	1	"As we gaze" to "institutions of a bankrupt Order." (*MBW, 102–103*)
57	17	"'*The winds of despair,*'" to "'*requirements of its maturity.*'" (*PDC, 121–123*)
62	3	"This is the stage which the world" to "summits of power and glory." (*PDC*, 126–129)